ABOUT THE

Author

MARY O.D. EXPERT IS AN EXPERIENCED ORGANIZATIONAL DEVELOPMENT CONSULTANT WITH A DEMONSTRATED HISTORY OF (DESIGNING &) DELIVERING TRAINING SESSIONS AND FACILITATING WORKSHOPS.

THOSE 2,000+ HOURS SPENT IN THE TRAINING ROOM (TOGETHER WITH PARTICIPANTS FROM ALL OVER THE WORLD) MADE HER RECOGNISE THAT (GOOD) PREPARATION MAKES 95% OF THE SESSION'S SUCCESS.

MARY IS HIGHLY APPRECIATED FOR HER EXCELLENT FACILITATION AND INSTRUCTIONAL DESIGN SKILLS, WHICH MADE HER REALIZE THE IMPORTANT CONTRIBUTION SHE COULD BRING BY GIVING ACCESS TO THE DOCUMENTS SHE USES ON A DAILY BASIS. SO... WHY NOT TAKING ADVANTAGE OF THIS?

HOW TO USE

This Book

SCHEDULING YOUR WORKFLOW IS IMPERATIVE IF YOU WANT TO BE IN CONTROL OF ANY TRAINING SESSION, NO MATTER WE TALK ABOUT AN ONLINE OR CLASSROOM SETTING.

THIS BOOK IS DEDICATED TO ALL THE PROFESSIONALS INVOLVED IN TRAINING DESIGN AND DELIVERY, NAMELY (CORPORATE) TRAINERS, L&D(/OD/HR-D) PROFESSIONALS AND ALL TYPES OF CONSULTANTS (INTERNAL & EXTERNAL).

IMPORTANT: CONDUCTING A NEEDS ASSESSMENT IS PRE-REQUISITE TO USING A WORKFLOW SCHEDULE. AUTHOR'S ADVICE: NEVER SKIP THIS STEP!

BESIDES THAT... NOTHING TO ADD. **YOU WILL FIGURE IT OUT!**

GRAB THE

Freebies

MARY ALWAYS STARTS HER SESSIONS BY OFFERING SOME SMALL
GIFTS THAT ARE UNHOPED FOR. SHE SAYS THAT THIS HELPS AT
QUICKLY BUILDING RELATIONSHIPS THAT WOULD HELP IN TRAINING
DELIVERY LATER ON.

MARY HAS PREPARED SOME FREE RESOURCES THAT COMPLEMENT
THIS BOOK AND COULD BENEFIT YOU AS WELL. ARE YOU IN?

IF SO, PLEASE DROP HER AN EMAIL AT:

maryodexpert@gmail.com

...AND LET HER KNOW ABOUT IT.

PLEASE PUT "**WFS TEMPLATE**" AS THE SUBJECT IN YOUR EMAIL, BUT
FEEL FREE TO GIVE A BIT OF YOUR PROFESSIONAL BACKGROUND IN
THE BODY OF YOUR MESSAGE.

TRAINING ☐ WORKSHOP ☐ OTHER ☐

Preparation

PROJECT NAME:
CLIENT:
DATE:

THINGS TO DO

☐ _____

_____

☐ _____

_____

☐ _____

_____

☐ _____

_____

NOTES

PROJECT NAME:

DATE:

Workflow Schedule

LEARNING OBJECTIVES

1.

2.

3.

CONTENT:	METHOD:	MATERIALS:	TIME

DAILY BUFFER:

Conclusions

_____

_____

_____

_____

_____

_____

_____

_____

_____

OTHER REMARKS

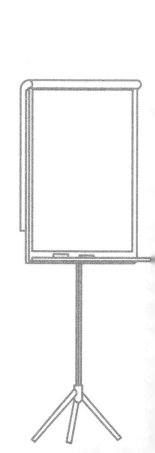

TRAINING ☐ WORKSHOP ☐ OTHER ☐

Preparation

PROJECT NAME:
CLIENT:
DATE:

THINGS TO DO

☐ _____

_____

☐ _____

_____

☐ _____

_____

☐ _____

_____

NOTES

PROJECT NAME: DATE:

 # Workflow Schedule

LEARNING OBJECTIVES

1.

2.

3.

CONTENT:	METHOD:	MATERIALS:	TIME

DAILY BUFFER:

Conclusions

_____

_____

_____

_____

_____

_____

_____

_____

_____

_____

OTHER REMARKS

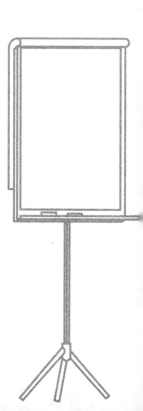

TRAINING ☐ WORKSHOP ☐ OTHER ☐

Preparation

PROJECT NAME:
CLIENT:
DATE:

THINGS TO DO

☐ _____

_____

☐ _____

_____

☐ _____

_____

☐ _____

_____

NOTES

PROJECT NAME: DATE:

# Workflow Schedule

LEARNING OBJECTIVES

1.

2.

3.

CONTENT:	METHOD:	MATERIALS:	TIME

                                              DAILY BUFFER:

# Conclusions

OTHER REMARKS

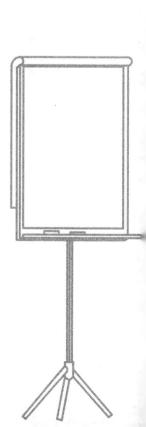

TRAINING ☐ WORKSHOP ☐ OTHER ☐

Preparation

PROJECT NAME:
CLIENT:
DATE:

THINGS TO DO

☐ _____

_____

☐ _____

_____

☐ _____

_____

☐ _____

_____

NOTES

PROJECT NAME: DATE:

 # Workflow Schedule

LEARNING OBJECTIVES

1.

2.

3.

CONTENT:	METHOD:	MATERIALS:	TIME

DAILY BUFFER:

Conclusions

OTHER REMARKS

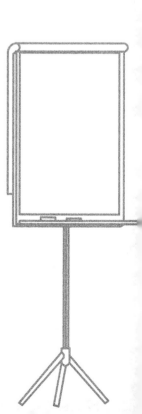

TRAINING ☐ WORKSHOP ☐ OTHER ☐

Preparation

PROJECT NAME:
CLIENT:
DATE:

THINGS TO DO

☐ _____

_____

☐ _____

_____

☐ _____

_____

☐ _____

_____

NOTES

PROJECT NAME: DATE:

 # *Workflow Schedule*

LEARNING OBJECTIVES

1.

2.

3.

CONTENT:	METHOD:	MATERIALS:	TIME

DAILY BUFFER:

Conclusions

OTHER REMARKS

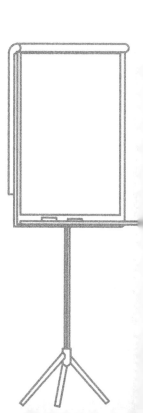

TRAINING ☐ WORKSHOP ☐ OTHER ☐

Preparation

PROJECT NAME:
CLIENT:
DATE:

THINGS TO DO

☐ _____

_____

☐ _____

_____

☐ _____

_____

☐ _____

_____

NOTES

PROJECT NAME: **DATE:**

Workflow Schedule

LEARNING OBJECTIVES

1.

2.

3.

CONTENT:	METHOD:	MATERIALS:	TIME

DAILY BUFFER:

Conclusions

OTHER REMARKS

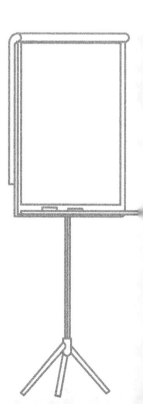

TRAINING ☐   WORKSHOP ☐   OTHER ☐

Preparation

PROJECT NAME:
CLIENT:
DATE:

THINGS TO DO

☐ _____

_____

☐ _____

_____

☐ _____

_____

☐ _____

_____

NOTES

PROJECT NAME: DATE:

 # Workflow Schedule

LEARNING OBJECTIVES

1.

2.

3.

CONTENT:	METHOD:	MATERIALS:	TIME

DAILY BUFFER:

Conclusions

_____

_____

_____

_____

_____

_____

_____

_____

_____

_____

OTHER REMARKS

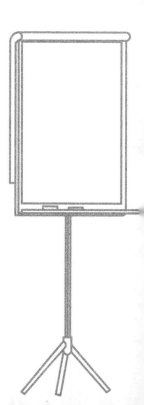

TRAINING ☐ WORKSHOP ☐ OTHER ☐

Preparation

PROJECT NAME:
CLIENT:
DATE:

THINGS TO DO

☐ _____

☐ _____

☐ _____

☐ _____

NOTES

PROJECT NAME: DATE:

 *Workflow Schedule*

___

LEARNING OBJECTIVES

1.

2.

3.

CONTENT:	METHOD:	MATERIALS:	TIME

DAILY BUFFER:

Conclusions

OTHER REMARKS

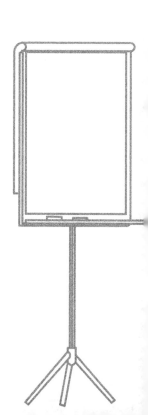

TRAINING ☐ WORKSHOP ☐ OTHER ☐

Preparation

PROJECT NAME:
CLIENT:
DATE:

THINGS TO DO

☐ _____

_____

☐ _____

_____

☐ _____

_____

☐ _____

_____

NOTES

PROJECT NAME: DATE:

 *Workflow Schedule*

LEARNING OBJECTIVES

1.

2.

3.

CONTENT:	METHOD:	MATERIALS:	TIME

DAILY BUFFER:

Conclusions

_____

_____

_____

_____

_____

_____

_____

_____

_____

_____

_____

OTHER REMARKS

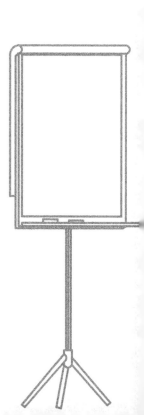

TRAINING ☐ WORKSHOP ☐ OTHER ☐

Preparation

PROJECT NAME:

CLIENT:

DATE:

THINGS TO DO

☐ _____

_____

☐ _____

_____

☐ _____

_____

☐ _____

_____

NOTES

PROJECT NAME: DATE:

Workflow Schedule

LEARNING OBJECTIVES

1.

2.

3.

CONTENT:	METHOD:	MATERIALS:	TIME

DAILY BUFFER:

Conclusions

OTHER REMARKS

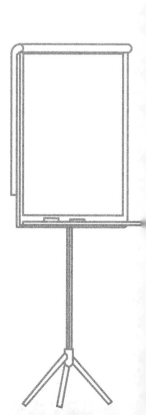

TRAINING ☐ WORKSHOP ☐ OTHER ☐

Preparation

PROJECT NAME:
CLIENT:
DATE:

THINGS TO DO

☐ _____

☐ _____

☐ _____

☐ _____

NOTES

PROJECT NAME: DATE:

 *Workflow Schedule*

LEARNING OBJECTIVES

1.

2.

3.

CONTENT:	METHOD:	MATERIALS:	TIME

DAILY BUFFER:

Conclusions

_____

_____

_____

_____

_____

_____

_____

_____

_____

_____

_____

OTHER REMARKS

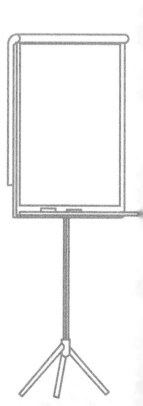

TRAINING ☐ WORKSHOP ☐ OTHER ☐

Preparation

PROJECT NAME:
CLIENT:
DATE:

THINGS TO DO

☐ _____

_____

☐ _____

_____

☐ _____

_____

☐ _____

_____

NOTES

PROJECT NAME: DATE:

 # Workflow Schedule

LEARNING OBJECTIVES

1.

2.

3.

CONTENT:	METHOD:	MATERIALS:	TIME

DAILY BUFFER:

Conclusions

_____

_____

_____

_____

_____

_____

_____

_____

_____

_____

OTHER REMARKS

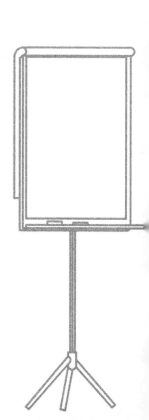

TRAINING ☐ WORKSHOP ☐ OTHER ☐

Preparation

PROJECT NAME:
CLIENT:
DATE:

THINGS TO DO

☐ _____

_____

☐ _____

_____

☐ _____

_____

☐ _____

_____

NOTES

PROJECT NAME: DATE:

# Workflow Schedule

LEARNING OBJECTIVES

1.

2.

3.

CONTENT:	METHOD:	MATERIALS:	TIME

DAILY BUFFER:

Conclusions

OTHER REMARKS

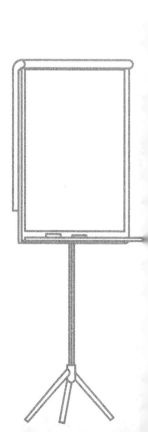

TRAINING ☐ WORKSHOP ☐ OTHER ☐

Preparation

PROJECT NAME:
CLIENT:
DATE:

THINGS TO DO

☐ _____

_____

☐ _____

_____

☐ _____

_____

☐ _____

_____

NOTES

PROJECT NAME: DATE:

 *Workflow Schedule*

_____

LEARNING OBJECTIVES

1.

2.

3.

CONTENT:	METHOD:	MATERIALS:	TIME

DAILY BUFFER:

Conclusions

_____

_____

_____

_____

_____

_____

_____

_____

_____

_____

_____

OTHER REMARKS

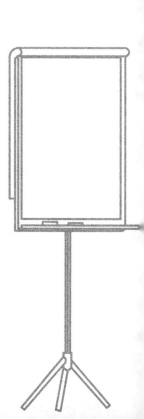

TRAINING ☐ WORKSHOP ☐ OTHER ☐

Preparation

PROJECT NAME:
CLIENT:
DATE:

THINGS TO DO

☐ _____

☐ _____

☐ _____

☐ _____

NOTES

PROJECT NAME: DATE:

 *Workflow Schedule*

LEARNING OBJECTIVES

1.

2.

3.

CONTENT:	METHOD:	MATERIALS:	TIME

DAILY BUFFER:

Conclusions

_____

_____

_____

_____

_____

_____

_____

_____

_____

_____

OTHER REMARKS

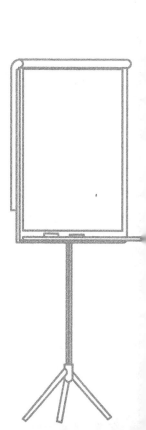

TRAINING ☐ WORKSHOP ☐ OTHER ☐

Preparation

PROJECT NAME:
CLIENT:
DATE:

THINGS TO DO

☐ _____

_____

☐ _____

_____

☐ _____

_____

☐ _____

_____

NOTES

PROJECT NAME: DATE:

 # Workflow Schedule

LEARNING OBJECTIVES

1.

2.

3.

CONTENT:	METHOD:	MATERIALS:	TIME

DAILY BUFFER:

# Conclusions

---

OTHER REMARKS

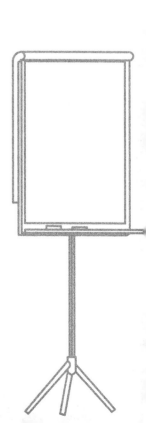

TRAINING ☐ WORKSHOP ☐ OTHER ☐

Preparation

PROJECT NAME:
CLIENT:
DATE:

THINGS TO DO

☐ _____

_____

☐ _____

_____

☐ _____

_____

☐ _____

_____

NOTES

PROJECT NAME: DATE:

 *Workflow Schedule*

LEARNING OBJECTIVES

1.

2.

3.

CONTENT:	METHOD:	MATERIALS:	TIME

DAILY BUFFER:

Conclusions

_____

_____

_____

_____

_____

_____

_____

_____

_____

_____

OTHER REMARKS

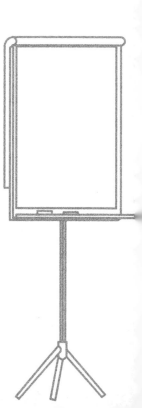

TRAINING ☐ WORKSHOP ☐ OTHER ☐

Preparation

PROJECT NAME:
CLIENT:
DATE:

THINGS TO DO

☐ _____

_____

☐ _____

_____

☐ _____

_____

☐ _____

_____

NOTES

PROJECT NAME: DATE:

Workflow Schedule

LEARNING OBJECTIVES

1.

2.

3.

CONTENT:	METHOD:	MATERIALS:	TIME

DAILY BUFFER:

Conclusions

OTHER REMARKS

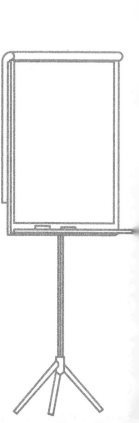

TRAINING ☐ WORKSHOP ☐ OTHER ☐

Preparation

PROJECT NAME:
CLIENT:
DATE:

THINGS TO DO

☐ _____

_____

☐ _____

_____

☐ _____

_____

☐ _____

_____

NOTES

PROJECT NAME: DATE:

Workflow Schedule

LEARNING OBJECTIVES

1.

2.

3.

CONTENT:	METHOD:	MATERIALS:	TIME

DAILY BUFFER:

Conclusions

_____

_____

_____

_____

_____

_____

_____

_____

_____

_____

OTHER REMARKS

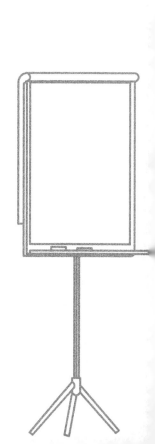

TRAINING ☐   WORKSHOP ☐   OTHER ☐

Preparation

PROJECT NAME:
CLIENT:
DATE:

THINGS TO DO

☐ _____

_____

☐ _____

_____

☐ _____

_____

☐ _____

_____

NOTES

PROJECT NAME: DATE:

Workflow Schedule

LEARNING OBJECTIVES
  1.

  2.

  3.

CONTENT:	METHOD:	MATERIALS:	TIME

DAILY BUFFER:

Conclusions

_____

_____

_____

_____

_____

_____

_____

_____

_____

_____

OTHER REMARKS

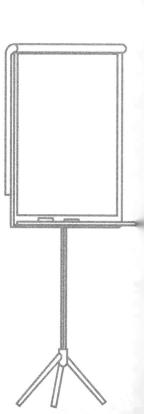

TRAINING ☐ WORKSHOP ☐ OTHER ☐

Preparation

PROJECT NAME:
CLIENT:
DATE:

THINGS TO DO

☐ _____

_____

☐ _____

_____

☐ _____

_____

☐ _____

_____

NOTES

PROJECT NAME: DATE:

 # Workflow Schedule

LEARNING OBJECTIVES

1.

2.

3.

CONTENT:	METHOD:	MATERIALS:	TIME

DAILY BUFFER:

Conclusions

_____

_____

_____

_____

_____

_____

_____

_____

_____

_____

OTHER REMARKS

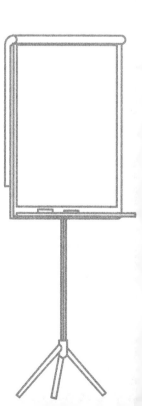

TRAINING ☐ WORKSHOP ☐ OTHER ☐

Preparation

PROJECT NAME:
CLIENT:
DATE:

THINGS TO DO

☐ _____

_____

☐ _____

_____

☐ _____

_____

☐ _____

_____

NOTES

PROJECT NAME: DATE:

Workflow Schedule

LEARNING OBJECTIVES

1.

2.

3.

CONTENT:	METHOD:	MATERIALS:	TIME

DAILY BUFFER:

Conclusions

OTHER REMARKS

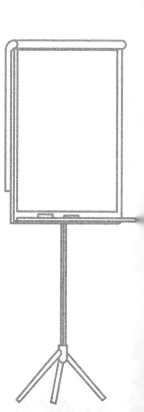

TRAINING ☐ WORKSHOP ☐ OTHER ☐

Preparation

PROJECT NAME:
CLIENT:
DATE:

THINGS TO DO

☐ _____

_____

☐ _____

_____

☐ _____

_____

☐ _____

_____

NOTES

PROJECT NAME: DATE:

 # Workflow Schedule

LEARNING OBJECTIVES

1.

2.

3.

CONTENT:	METHOD:	MATERIALS:	TIME

DAILY BUFFER:

Conclusions

_____

_____

_____

_____

_____

_____

_____

_____

_____

_____

OTHER REMARKS

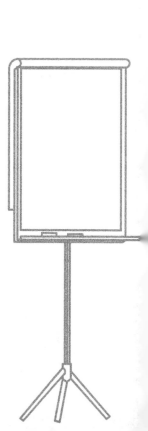

TRAINING ☐ WORKSHOP ☐ OTHER ☐

Preparation

PROJECT NAME:
CLIENT:
DATE:

THINGS TO DO

☐ _____

_____

☐ _____

_____

☐ _____

_____

☐ _____

_____

NOTES

PROJECT NAME: DATE:

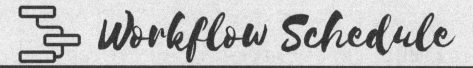 # Workflow Schedule

LEARNING OBJECTIVES

1.

2.

3.

CONTENT:	METHOD:	MATERIALS:	TIME

DAILY BUFFER:

Conclusions

_____

_____

_____

_____

_____

_____

_____

_____

_____

_____

OTHER REMARKS

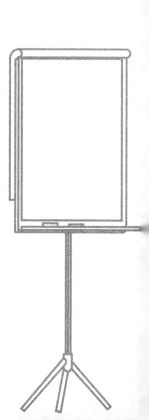

TRAINING ☐ WORKSHOP ☐ OTHER ☐

Preparation

PROJECT NAME:
CLIENT:
DATE:

THINGS TO DO

☐ _____

☐ _____

☐ _____

☐ _____

NOTES

PROJECT NAME: DATE:

 *Workflow Schedule*

LEARNING OBJECTIVES

1.

2.

3.

CONTENT:	METHOD:	MATERIALS:	TIME

DAILY BUFFER:

Conclusions

OTHER REMARKS

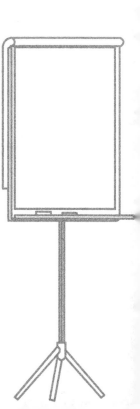

TRAINING ☐   WORKSHOP ☐   OTHER ☐

Preparation

PROJECT NAME:
CLIENT:
DATE:

THINGS TO DO

☐ _____

_____

☐ _____

_____

☐ _____

_____

☐ _____

_____

NOTES

PROJECT NAME: DATE:

Workflow Schedule

LEARNING OBJECTIVES

1.

2.

3.

CONTENT:	METHOD:	MATERIALS:	TIME

DAILY BUFFER:

Conclusions

_____

_____

_____

_____

_____

_____

_____

_____

_____

_____

OTHER REMARKS

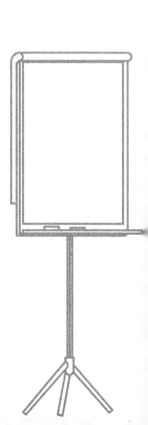

TRAINING ☐ WORKSHOP ☐ OTHER ☐

Preparation

PROJECT NAME:
CLIENT:
DATE:

THINGS TO DO

☐ _____

_____

☐ _____

_____

☐ _____

_____

☐ _____

_____

NOTES

PROJECT NAME: DATE:

 *Workflow Schedule*

LEARNING OBJECTIVES

1.

2.

3.

CONTENT:	METHOD:	MATERIALS:	TIME

DAILY BUFFER:

Conclusions

_____

_____

_____

_____

_____

_____

_____

_____

_____

_____

OTHER REMARKS

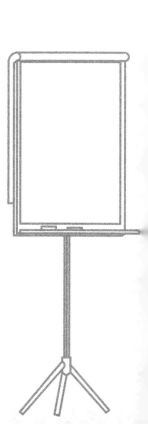

TRAINING ☐ WORKSHOP ☐ OTHER ☐

Preparation

PROJECT NAME:
CLIENT:
DATE:

THINGS TO DO

☐ _____

_____

☐ _____

_____

☐ _____

_____

☐ _____

_____

NOTES

PROJECT NAME: DATE:

 *Workflow Schedule*

LEARNING OBJECTIVES

1.

2.

3.

CONTENT:	METHOD:	MATERIALS:	TIME

DAILY BUFFER:

Conclusions

_____

_____

_____

_____

_____

_____

_____

_____

_____

_____

OTHER REMARKS

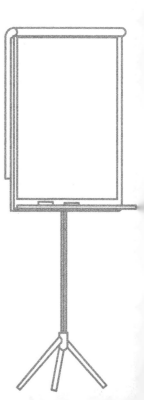

TRAINING ☐ WORKSHOP ☐ OTHER ☐

Preparation

PROJECT NAME:
CLIENT:
DATE:

THINGS TO DO

☐ _____

_____

☐ _____

_____

☐ _____

_____

☐ _____

_____

NOTES

PROJECT NAME: DATE:

Workflow Schedule

LEARNING OBJECTIVES

1.

2.

3.

CONTENT:	METHOD:	MATERIALS:	TIME

DAILY BUFFER:

Conclusions

_____

_____

_____

_____

_____

_____

_____

_____

_____

_____

OTHER REMARKS

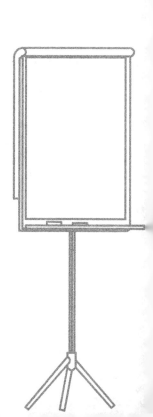

TRAINING ☐ WORKSHOP ☐ OTHER ☐

Preparation

PROJECT NAME:
CLIENT:
DATE:

THINGS TO DO

☐ _____

_____

☐ _____

_____

☐ _____

_____

☐ _____

_____

NOTES

PROJECT NAME: DATE:

 *Workflow Schedule*

LEARNING OBJECTIVES

1.

2.

3.

CONTENT:	METHOD:	MATERIALS:	TIME

DAILY BUFFER:

Conclusions

OTHER REMARKS

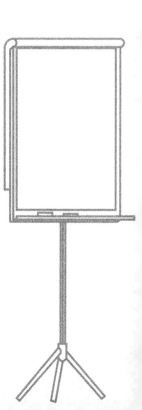

TRAINING ☐ WORKSHOP ☐ OTHER ☐

Preparation

PROJECT NAME:
CLIENT:
DATE:

THINGS TO DO

☐ _____

_____

☐ _____

_____

☐ _____

_____

☐ _____

_____

NOTES

PROJECT NAME: DATE:

 # *Workflow Schedule*

LEARNING OBJECTIVES

1.

2.

3.

CONTENT:	METHOD:	MATERIALS:	TIME

DAILY BUFFER:

Conclusions

_____

_____

_____

_____

_____

_____

_____

_____

_____

_____

_____

OTHER REMARKS

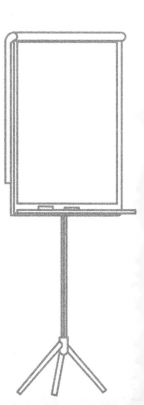

TRAINING ☐ WORKSHOP ☐ OTHER ☐

Preparation

PROJECT NAME:
CLIENT:
DATE:

THINGS TO DO

☐ _____

_____

☐ _____

_____

☐ _____

_____

☐ _____

_____

NOTES

PROJECT NAME: DATE:

Workflow Schedule

LEARNING OBJECTIVES

1.

2.

3.

CONTENT:	METHOD:	MATERIALS:	TIME

DAILY BUFFER:

Conclusions

_____

_____

_____

_____

_____

_____

_____

_____

_____

_____

OTHER REMARKS

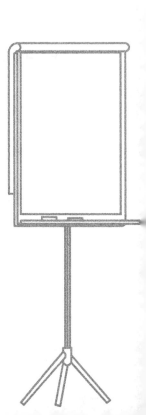

TRAINING ☐ WORKSHOP ☐ OTHER ☐

Preparation

PROJECT NAME:
CLIENT:
DATE:

THINGS TO DO

☐ _____

_____

☐ _____

_____

☐ _____

_____

☐ _____

_____

NOTES

PROJECT NAME: DATE:

 *Workflow Schedule*

LEARNING OBJECTIVES

1.

2.

3.

CONTENT:	METHOD:	MATERIALS:	TIME

DAILY BUFFER:

Conclusions

OTHER REMARKS

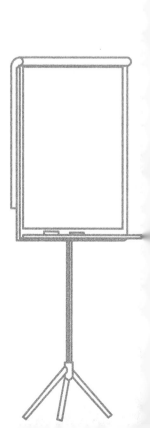

TRAINING ☐ WORKSHOP ☐ OTHER ☐

Preparation

PROJECT NAME:
CLIENT:
DATE:

THINGS TO DO

☐ _____

_____

☐ _____

_____

☐ _____

_____

☐ _____

_____

NOTES

PROJECT NAME: DATE:

 *Workflow Schedule*

LEARNING OBJECTIVES

1.

2.

3.

CONTENT:	METHOD:	MATERIALS:	TIME

DAILY BUFFER:

Conclusions

OTHER REMARKS

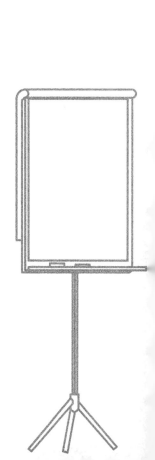

TRAINING ☐ WORKSHOP ☐ OTHER ☐

Preparation

PROJECT NAME:
CLIENT:
DATE:

THINGS TO DO

☐ _____

_____

☐ _____

_____

☐ _____

_____

☐ _____

_____

NOTES

PROJECT NAME: DATE:

 *Workflow Schedule*

LEARNING OBJECTIVES

1.

2.

3.

CONTENT:	METHOD:	MATERIALS:	TIME

DAILY BUFFER:

Conclusions

_____

_____

_____

_____

_____

_____

_____

_____

_____

_____

_____

OTHER REMARKS

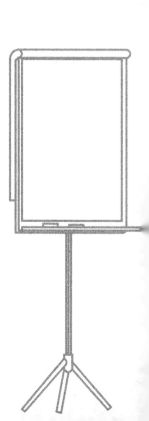

TRAINING ☐ WORKSHOP ☐ OTHER ☐

Preparation

PROJECT NAME:
CLIENT:
DATE:

THINGS TO DO

☐ _____

_____

☐ _____

_____

☐ _____

_____

☐ _____

_____

NOTES

PROJECT NAME: DATE:

 # Workflow Schedule

LEARNING OBJECTIVES

1.

2.

3.

CONTENT:	METHOD:	MATERIALS:	TIME

DAILY BUFFER:

Conclusions

_____

_____

_____

_____

_____

_____

_____

_____

_____

_____

OTHER REMARKS

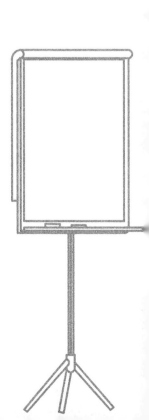

TRAINING ☐ WORKSHOP ☐ OTHER ☐

Preparation

PROJECT NAME:
CLIENT:
DATE:

THINGS TO DO

☐ _____

_____

☐ _____

_____

☐ _____

_____

☐ _____

_____

NOTES

PROJECT NAME: DATE:

 *Workflow Schedule*

LEARNING OBJECTIVES

1.

2.

3.

CONTENT:	METHOD:	MATERIALS:	TIME

DAILY BUFFER:

Conclusions

OTHER REMARKS

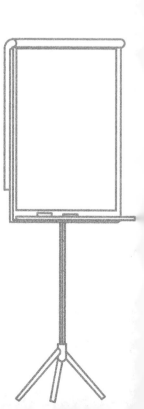

TRAINING ☐ WORKSHOP ☐ OTHER ☐

Preparation

PROJECT NAME:
CLIENT:
DATE:

THINGS TO DO

☐ _____

_____

☐ _____

_____

☐ _____

_____

☐ _____

_____

NOTES

PROJECT NAME: DATE:

LEARNING OBJECTIVES

1.

2.

3.

CONTENT:	METHOD:	MATERIALS:	TIME

DAILY BUFFER:

Conclusions

_____

_____

_____

_____

_____

_____

_____

_____

_____

_____

OTHER REMARKS

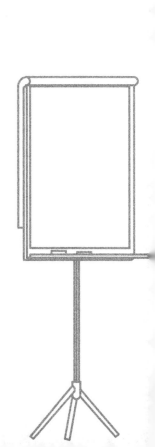

TRAINING ☐ WORKSHOP ☐ OTHER ☐

Preparation

PROJECT NAME:
CLIENT:
DATE:

THINGS TO DO

☐ _____

_____

☐ _____

_____

☐ _____

_____

☐ _____

_____

NOTES

PROJECT NAME: DATE:

 *Workflow Schedule*

LEARNING OBJECTIVES

1.

2.

3.

CONTENT:	METHOD:	MATERIALS:	TIME

DAILY BUFFER:

Conclusions

_____

_____

_____

_____

_____

_____

_____

_____

_____

_____

OTHER REMARKS

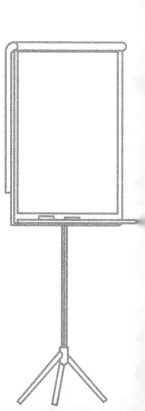

TRAINING ☐   WORKSHOP ☐   OTHER ☐

Preparation

PROJECT NAME:
CLIENT:
DATE:

THINGS TO DO

☐ _____

_____

☐ _____

_____

☐ _____

_____

☐ _____

_____

NOTES

PROJECT NAME: DATE:

 # Workflow Schedule

LEARNING OBJECTIVES

1.

2.

3.

CONTENT:	METHOD:	MATERIALS:	TIME

DAILY BUFFER:

Conclusions

_____

_____

_____

_____

_____

_____

_____

_____

_____

_____

_____

OTHER REMARKS

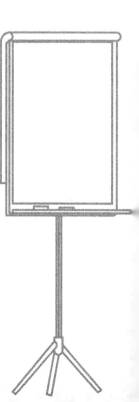

TRAINING ☐ WORKSHOP ☐ OTHER ☐

Preparation

PROJECT NAME:
CLIENT:
DATE:

THINGS TO DO

☐ _____

☐ _____

☐ _____

☐ _____

NOTES

PROJECT NAME: DATE:

 *Workflow Schedule*

LEARNING OBJECTIVES

1.

2.

3.

CONTENT:	METHOD:	MATERIALS:	TIME

DAILY BUFFER:

Conclusions

OTHER REMARKS

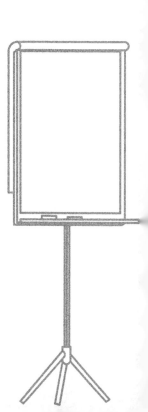

TRAINING ☐ WORKSHOP ☐ OTHER ☐

Preparation

PROJECT NAME:
CLIENT:
DATE:

THINGS TO DO

☐ _____

_____

☐ _____

_____

☐ _____

_____

☐ _____

_____

NOTES

PROJECT NAME: DATE:

 *Workflow Schedule*

LEARNING OBJECTIVES

1.

2.

3.

CONTENT:	METHOD:	MATERIALS:	TIME

DAILY BUFFER:

Conclusions

OTHER REMARKS

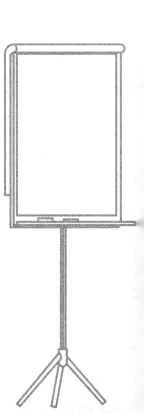

TRAINING ☐ WORKSHOP ☐ OTHER ☐

Preparation

PROJECT NAME:
CLIENT:
DATE:

THINGS TO DO

☐ _____

_____

☐ _____

_____

☐ _____

_____

☐ _____

_____

NOTES

PROJECT NAME: **DATE:**

 *Workflow Schedule*

LEARNING OBJECTIVES

1.

2.

3.

CONTENT:	METHOD:	MATERIALS:	TIME

DAILY BUFFER:

Conclusions

_____

_____

_____

_____

_____

_____

_____

_____

_____

_____

OTHER REMARKS

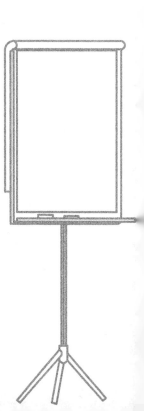

TRAINING ☐ WORKSHOP ☐ OTHER ☐

Preparation

PROJECT NAME:
CLIENT:
DATE:

THINGS TO DO

☐ _____

_____

☐ _____

_____

☐ _____

_____

☐ _____

_____

NOTES

PROJECT NAME: DATE:

 *Workflow Schedule*

LEARNING OBJECTIVES

1.

2.

3.

CONTENT:	METHOD:	MATERIALS:	TIME

DAILY BUFFER:

Conclusions

_____

_____

_____

_____

_____

_____

_____

_____

_____

_____

OTHER REMARKS

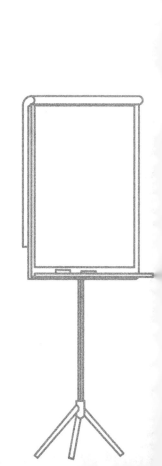

TRAINING ☐ WORKSHOP ☐ OTHER ☐

Preparation

PROJECT NAME:
CLIENT:
DATE:

THINGS TO DO

☐ _____

_____

☐ _____

_____

☐ _____

_____

☐ _____

_____

NOTES

Workflow Schedule

LEARNING OBJECTIVES

1.

2.

3.

CONTENT:	METHOD:	MATERIALS:	TIME

DAILY BUFFER:

Conclusions

OTHER REMARKS

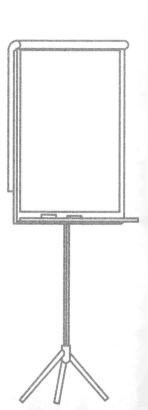

TRAINING ☐   WORKSHOP ☐   OTHER ☐

Preparation

PROJECT NAME:
CLIENT:
DATE:

THINGS TO DO

☐ _____

_____

☐ _____

_____

☐ _____

_____

☐ _____

_____

NOTES

PROJECT NAME: **DATE:**

 *Workflow Schedule*

LEARNING OBJECTIVES

1.

2.

3.

CONTENT:	METHOD:	MATERIALS:	TIME

DAILY BUFFER:

Conclusions

_____

_____

_____

_____

_____

_____

_____

_____

_____

_____

OTHER REMARKS

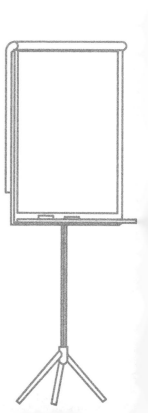

TRAINING ☐   WORKSHOP ☐   OTHER ☐

Preparation

PROJECT NAME:
CLIENT:
DATE:

THINGS TO DO

☐ _____

_____

☐ _____

_____

☐ _____

_____

☐ _____

_____

NOTES

PROJECT NAME: DATE:

Workflow Schedule

LEARNING OBJECTIVES

1.

2.

3.

CONTENT:	METHOD:	MATERIALS:	TIME

DAILY BUFFER:

Conclusions

OTHER REMARKS

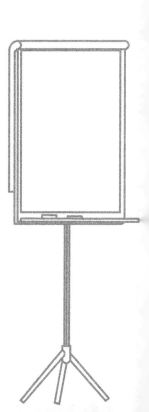

TRAINING ☐   WORKSHOP ☐   OTHER ☐

Preparation

PROJECT NAME:
CLIENT:
DATE:

THINGS TO DO

☐ _____

_____

☐ _____

_____

☐ _____

_____

☐ _____

_____

NOTES

PROJECT NAME: DATE:

 *Workflow Schedule*

LEARNING OBJECTIVES

1.

2.

3.

CONTENT:	METHOD:	MATERIALS:	TIME

DAILY BUFFER:

Conclusions

OTHER REMARKS

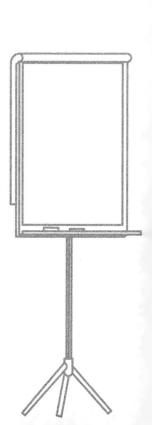

TRAINING ☐ WORKSHOP ☐ OTHER ☐

Preparation

PROJECT NAME:
CLIENT:
DATE:

THINGS TO DO

☐ _____

_____

☐ _____

_____

☐ _____

_____

☐ _____

_____

NOTES

PROJECT NAME: DATE:

Workflow Schedule

LEARNING OBJECTIVES

1.

2.

3.

CONTENT:	METHOD:	MATERIALS:	TIME

DAILY BUFFER:

Conclusions

_____

_____

_____

_____

_____

_____

_____

_____

_____

_____

OTHER REMARKS

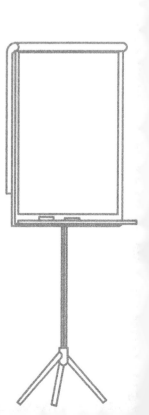

TRAINING ☐ WORKSHOP ☐ OTHER ☐

Preparation

PROJECT NAME:
CLIENT:
DATE:

THINGS TO DO

☐ _____

☐ _____

☐ _____

☐ _____

NOTES

PROJECT NAME: DATE:

Workflow Schedule

LEARNING OBJECTIVES

1.

2.

3.

CONTENT:	METHOD:	MATERIALS:	TIME

DAILY BUFFER:

Conclusions

OTHER REMARKS

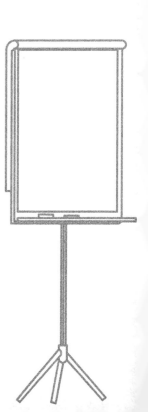